Smart Starters

Vocabulary

Motivational Exercises to Stimulate the Brain

by Marjorie Frank

Incentive Publications
Nashville, Tennessee

Illustrated by Marta Drayton
Cover by Geoffrey Brittingham
Edited by Jill S. Norris

ISBN 0-86530-079-8

1   2   3   4   5   6   7   8   9   10   08   07   06   05

PRINTED IN THE UNITED STATES OF AMERICA
www.incentivepublications.com

Table of Contents

Introduction

What is a Smart Starter?

A Smart Starter changes "extra" moments in a classroom setting into teachable moments. They are designed to take short amounts of time. However, Smart Starters are NOT short on substance. The Smart Starters in this book are packed full of important skills to practice and polish or to reinforce and extend.

When are Smart Starters used?

As their name suggests, they are good for igniting learning. Instead of the slow move into a class period, lesson, or school day, a Smart Starter quick-starts the action. Each one warms up the brain with a sparkling challenge. Students also need this kind of spark at times other than the beginning of the day or class period. Use a Smart Starter any time there is a lull, or any time students need a break from a longer activity. They work effectively to stimulate thinking at the beginning, end, or middle of a class period, or any other time you can squeeze in an extra ten minutes.

Why use Smart Starters?

They're energizing! They're stimulating! They're fun! They nudge students to focus on a specific goal while "waking up" tired minds. They require students to make use of previously acquired knowledge and skills. Because of their short length, they insure quick success and quick rewards—thus inspiring confidence and satisfaction for the learners.

How to Use This Book . . .

Kick-Off a New Unit

The starters are grouped by general topics and skill areas. One or more of them might help to ease students into a new area of study. For instance, start off your unit on learning new words with *Invitation To A Brouhaha* (page 9) or *Words With Attitude* (page 16).

Spark a Longer Lesson

Any of these short activities can be expanded. A starter may inspire your students to develop questions or examples along the same lines—expanding the warm-up into a full-blown vocabulary lesson.

Review a Concept

Dust off those rusty skills with a Smart Starter. For instance: Have your students been away from the study of word structure for a while? Refresh and deepen what they know about word parts with *The Heart of a Word* (page 42) or *Pass It On To Add On* (page 48).

Charge-Up Thinking Skills & Ignite Creativity

The Smart Starters are not only for language arts class. Use them **any** time to stimulate minds. Doing a Smart Starter will sharpen thinking processes and challenge brains. In addition, Smart Starters work well as starting points for students to create other similar questions and problems.

Invitation to a Brouhaha

Brouhaha: What a wonderful word! It will take only a short time to help students get to know this word well enough to remember it forever.

What is a *brouhaha*? Ask students to find out. Then, they can work in pairs to . . .

- Think up and describe (orally) three situations in which a ***brouhaha*** could develop.

- Make a list of ten things a person could do to avoid a ***brouhaha***.

- Think of the names of two fictitious characters that might be involved in a ***brouhaha***.

- Write 20 words that might be used in a description of a ***brouhaha***.

Words with Pizzazz

Besides beginning with the letter **P**, these particular words have punch! Write them on the board and supply students with dictionaries. Give them these questions orally or in writing.

1. Your Aunt Maude is ***persnickety*** about healthy eating. She eats three chocolate bars a day. Is this a ***paradox***?

2. Tomorrow you are having a meeting with your accountant in his tiny office. You have learned that he has a ***paunch*** and ***pertussis***. Which is more worrisome to you? Why?

3. You've heard a rumor that a hiking partner has ***pernicious*** thoughts about you. Should you change your plans for a hike with her along the ***precipice*** above the river?

4. You've learned that you need some eye surgery. Should you choose a surgeon who is ***pugnacious*** or ***punctilious***?

pernicious
punctilious
precipice
paunch
pugnacious
paradox
persnickety
pertussis

Ten Things

Have students get to know a new word well by creating a **"Top 10"** list for it. They may work in small groups or individually to write lists of 10 things related to each of these words.

Top 10 Things *that Should be* **Alleviated**	Top 10 Things *Never to* **Squander**	Top 10 Things *to* **Mollify**	Top 10 Things *that are* **Gossamer**
————	————	————	————
————	————	————	————
————	————	————	————
————	————	————	————
————	————	————	————
————	————	————	————
————	————	————	————
————	————	————	————

Choose with Caution

For each question, there is a choice to make. Once the meanings of the words are known, the choice will be easier. Give students a copy of the eight questions. They should use a dictionary to help them sort out the word meanings.

1. Your mom starts a lecture about cleaning your room. Do you hope she is *laconic* or *loquacious*?

2. You just finished a difficult job. Would you like to be *lauded* or *rebuked*?

3. At the end of a long day of school, would you rather have a *repast* or a *flogging*?

4. You're moving to a new house. Would you rather it be *commodious* or *dank*?

5. Your friend invites you over for supper. Do you hope the meal is *meager* or *sumptuous*?

6. After walking across town to the movies, do you hope the theater is *temperate* or *sweltering*?

7. Your waiter is balancing six sundaes on his tray. Would you rather he be *adroit* or *incompetent*?

8. You're opening a bank account. Would you like the bank manager to be *scrupulous* or *furtive*?

"Painted" Words

Painting a word can fix the meaning of the word in students' minds forever. To *paint* a word, a student first learns the meaning, then writes the letters of the word in a shape that shows the word's meaning.

Students can choose one or more of these words to paint, depending on the time available. Use colored markers, crayons, colored chalk, or colored pencils to "paint" each word.

ample   minimize   serpentine   spritz   whorl

ornate   erratic   recline   grovel

serrated   undulate   circular

Example: CONGLOMERATION

Careless Quotes

Each of these quotes has a word that is used incorrectly. How careless of the speaker! Read the quotes aloud and ask students to identify the word that is not quite right. They should find the meaning of that word and explain why it does not fit in the sentence.

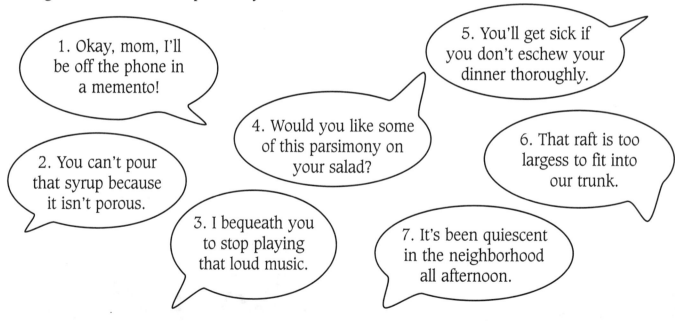

1. Okay, mom, I'll be off the phone in a memento!

2. You can't pour that syrup because it isn't porous.

3. I bequeath you to stop playing that loud music.

4. Would you like some of this parsimony on your salad?

5. You'll get sick if you don't eschew your dinner thoroughly.

6. That raft is too largess to fit into our trunk.

7. It's been quiescent in the neighborhood all afternoon.

Talk About In & Out

Dozens of interesting words begin with IN or OUT. These are a few that students might not know. Divide the class into groups of four. Give a copy of the two word lists to each group. Two of the students should find the meanings of the IN words. The other two can find the meanings of the OUT words.

Each pair explains their words to the other pair in the group. The four group members use the new words in a sentence. When the activity is finished, all the people in all the groups should be familiar with all the words.

IN

infinitesimal
inexplicable
inopportune
incite
inundate
invective

OUT

outflank
outlay
outface
outmoded
outlier
outage

Words with Attitude

Each of these words suggests a certain attitude. Give every student one of these words. After they understand the meaning of the word, they can draw a character who has that attitude.

effete   *pugnacious*

dour   *churlish*

erudite   *languid*

demure   *jocund*

outrageous   *dynamic*

inquisitive   *disdainful*

Example:

Haughty

Mini-Mysteries

Writing a mystery using new words helps students remember word meanings. Ask students to choose one of the pairs of words and to write a brief mystery that includes both words. Find time to share the mysteries so that others can guess at the meanings of the two words.

liege — insolent   **expedient — crepe**

martinet — disparage   **bonanza — matinee**

puce — soffit   **illuminated — pullet**

derelict — sleuth   **ocelot — mythic**

pragmatic — fauna   **aquatic — schematic**

Example:

The Mystery of the Missing Diva

The *prima donna* finished her morning rehearsal at 11:30 AM. The whole opera house quivered with the vibrations from her powerful *warbling*, and the workers setting up the sets left for lunch with their ears ringing. She headed for her dressing room and has not been seen since. How can the show possibly go on tonight without her singing the lead role?

Where Are You?

Each of these *Q* words names a place or situation where a person might be. Divide students into small groups. Give each group one of these words. Group members discover what the word means and work together to answer the questions about the word.

quandary	**quarry**	**quadrant**
quagmire	**quadrangle**	**quatrain**
quay	**quartet**	**queue**

You are in a _____. Where are you?
(fill in the Q word)

What is it like to be there?

What might you be doing?

Why are you there?

Give time for groups to share their descriptions with the whole class.

Take Five

Take Five can be used with any five new words. Give students the words and these five tasks. After students find the words' meanings, they do the tasks.

momentous   reproof   mariner

trivial   elude

1. Identify the part of speech for each word.

2. Identify two words that have **opposite** meanings.

3. Write a question that contains three of the words.

4. Give a statement of advice that contains two of the words.

5. Identify one structural feature that all five words have in common.

Words to Stir the Senses

If students dig deep into their dictionaries and experiences for examples to match these words with high "sense" appeal, they'll add the words to their vocabularies.

Read these directions to students. They may work in small groups to complete the tasks.

Learn the meanings of these two mouth-watering words: ***pungent*** and ***piquant***.

- Prepare a short café menu containing only items that are *pungent* and/or *piquant*.

These two words will stimulate the senses differently: ***viscous*** and ***repugnant***.
Find their meanings.

- Create a short deli menu containing only items that are *viscous* and/or *repugnant*.

       Copyright ©2005 by Incentive Publications, Inc., Nashville, TN.

Best Friends

This game will help students learn some new words that are great for describing people. Give each student the name of one "best friend." The assignment is to learn the meaning of the bold describing word, state the name of the best friend, and tell something about that friend that shows an understanding of the new vocabulary word.

Example: My new best friend is Extemporaneous Ed. Since I met Ed, I always need to be ready to do something unexpected on the spur of the moment.

1. **Contentious** Connie

2. **Sagacious** Sam

3. **Impudent** Ira

4. **Derisive** Della

5. **Giddy** Gabe

6. **Tenacious** Tom

7. **Mettlesome** Moe

8. **Cantankerous** Christie

9. **Blithe** Bob

10. **Vacillating** Val

11. **Fastidious** Flo

12. **Gregarious** George

Abundant Creations

Learn the word ***prolific***. This activity considers sources of prolific creations. Ask students to find the meanings of ***prolific*** and ***proliferate***. Enjoy brainstorming names to fill these lists.

Prolific Authors	Prolific Songwriters	Prolific Inventors	Prolific Plants	Prolific Painters
1. _____	1. _____	1. _____	1. _____	1. _____
2. _____	2. _____	2. _____	2. _____	2. _____
3. _____	3. _____	3. _____	3. _____	3. _____
4. _____	4. _____	4. _____	4. _____	4. _____
5. _____	5. _____	5. _____	5. _____	5. _____

Words on the Move

These words all have something to do with motion. Students can find out what kind of motion and draw a line that shows or suggests the motion for each word.

diffuse   reflect   inundate   veer

trudge   jostle   slither   stride

glide   weave

agitate   plummet

meander

One Word, Many Meanings

Divide these words among students and challenge them to show (by telling, drawing, writing sentences, or demonstrating) at least 3 meanings for each word.

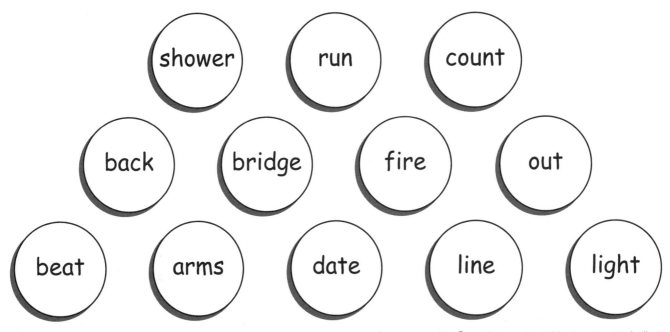

shower   run   count   back   bridge   fire   out   beat   arms   date   line   light

What's Up?

Share the story with students by reading it to them. Ask them to listen for different uses of the word **up**. They can count the number of different uses they hear. When the story is finished, ask them to think of 10–20 different additional uses.

My mom got up on the wrong side of the bed this morning. I think it's because all of us were stirring up trouble last night and she went to bed upset. Today, she got all up in arms because I put on a lot of her make-up and dressed up the dog in her nightgown. Pretty soon, I was sent up to my room to think up an apology. I climbed up in my bed and opened up my favorite book and got caught up in a good story. It took up about an hour. Then I closed up the book and got up the courage to go back downstairs where I cleaned up the kitchen and worked up the nerve to see what Mom was up to. I stood up straight and greeted her cheerfully: "Hey Mom!" I said. "What's up?"

Comfortable Surroundings

The **context** of a word is the setting in which the word is found. Often the context gives a reader or listener clues to the meaning of a word. Read a sentence to the class. Name the bolded word. Ask students to listen and use the surrounding words to discover the meaning of that word. Read the sentence again.

1. **terse** — Mom's scolding was ***terse***. It only took thirty seconds, and there was no mistaking the point she was making.

2. **beguiled** — Many young actors have been ***beguiled*** into believing they could become famous movie stars—only to be sorely disappointed.

3. **imminent** — Don't leave the boarding area because the plane's departure is ***imminent***.

4. **feigned** — Jana ***feigned*** surprise even though she knew her friends were throwing her a birthday party.

Give the words below to a pair of students. Ask them to work together to create the "surroundings" that will reveal the words' meanings.

uncanny – ethereal – aberration – admonish – coerce
rancid – callous – flippant – divulge – figment
sever – lucid – mire – rambunctious – portent

Words that Confuse

Some words sound so much like other words that it's hard to tell them apart. But, it's important to know the difference between them; otherwise, students may use the wrong word in the wrong place! Give students the 8 pairs of words and the questions. They'll need to use their dictionaries to choose the right answers.

1. **allude – elude** Which do you need to do in a dangerous situation?

2. **credible – credulous** Which kind of person is easier to trick?

3. **elicit – illicit** Which might describe a law-breaker's act?

4. **precipitant – precipitous** Which could describe an unpredictable teenager?

5. **ravage – ravish** Which might describe the actions of a hurricane?

6. **legato – staccato** Which is smooth?

7. **tortuous – torturous** Which is twisty?

8. **nefarious – notorious** Which kind of person is most likely NOT to be trustworthy?

Not Too Close to Call

These words may seem too close to call, but if the students are sharp (and if they have dictionaries handy), they can tell the difference. Try this as an oral exercise to see how quickly the class can answer all the questions correctly.

1. C. J. gives half of her allowance to her little sister.   *Is she **benevolent** or **belligerent**?*

2. Mike made a $3000 profit when he sold his convertible.
   *Was the deal **lucrative** or **luminous**?*

3. Dad gave a loud lecture when we broke his power tools.
   *Was this a **tirade** or a **treacle**?*

4. The friendship ended in a bitter argument.   *Was this **acrid** or **acrimonious**?*

5. That massage really fixed my backache.   *Was the pain **affiliated** or **alleviated**?*

6. These mosquitoes are everywhere!   *Are they **unctuous** or **ubiquitous**?*

More Than a Definition

> The **denotation** of a word is its dictionary definition.
>
> The **connotation** of a word is all the ideas and images suggested by the word, and may be different for different people.

Read each *denotation*, and let students discuss it until they agree on what the word is. Have them brainstorm ideas and impressions about the *connotation* of the word.

1. a rotating column of air accompanied by a funnel-shaped downward whirling cloud
2. a fictional character who is at odds with or in opposition to the hero of the story
3. very little or no light
4. unwell
5. to express mirthful sounds with the mouth open in a wide smile
6. an adjective pertaining to something (such as a living being) from the planet Mars
7. to seize by force
8. a conical wafer holding a creamy, frozen dessert

Matchmaking

Get students on their feet to match up some synonyms. Write each word on a card (accompanied by the number). Pin a card on each student. Students find the meanings of their words and then form synonym pairs.

1. illusory	11. blame	21. malice
2. macabre	12. salubrious	22. onus
3. deride	13. ridicule	23. scrupulous
4. jocose	14. nickname	24. languid
5. conscientious	15. piebald	25. imaginary
6. docile	16. gruesome	26. spotted
7. rebuke	17. convivial	27. wholesome
8. excess	18. upbraid	28. submissive
9. rancor	19. refined	29. moniker
10. listless	20. plethora	30. urbane

Who's the Pretender?

All the words, except one, in each numbered group below have similar meanings. This one is an imposter—falsely pretending to be a synonym. Give one group of words and a dictionary to each pair of students. Ask them to find the meanings and identify the pretender in the group.

1. paltry   shoddy   shabby   troublesome
2. irascible   placid   irate   wrathful
3. voracious   guileful   insidious   cunning
4. tact   flair   finesse   subtlety
5. frenetic   frantic   frenzied   finicky
6. insolent   insulting   insouciant   presumptuous
7. emprise   emit   radiate   ooze
8. chafe   vex   tease   irritate
9. pacify   suppress   quell   quibble
10. vacuous   inane   vapid   silly

Picture This!

Give each student a word from the list below. Challenge each student to find the meaning of the word, write the word, write a synonym for the word, and draw a picture that is connected to the word in some way or somehow shows its meaning—in just 10 minutes!

abrasive	esteem	palpitate
beleaguered	exorbitant	paraphernalia
cache	glower	rend
copious	interloper	sanguine
depreciate	mesmerized	torpor
dupe	mottled	unkempt

Synonym Scramble

Ten pairs of synonyms are scrambled on this grid. Give the grid to teams of 3–4 students. Each team has ten minutes to find the pairs of words that match (synonyms). They'll probably need dictionaries!

1 parsimonious	2 rabble	3 pugnacious	4 lout	5 parity
6 peccadillo	7 beguile	8 impasse	9 stalemate	10 swarm
11 disconsolate	12 penurious	13 humdrum	14 enthrall	15 desolate
16 contentious	17 equality	18 burl	19 stodgy	20 fault

Speaking in Opposites

These speakers are saying the opposite of what they really mean. Have students find the mistake in each statement and replace it with an antonym that will make the statement sensible.

"I'm so sorry that I was rude to you. I beg your ~~chastisement.~~" *pardon*

1. "The puzzle was so enigmatic that a 5-year-old could solve it!"

4. "Please take your seats and quiet down so that we can terminate this meeting."

3. "We decided to elect Joe as the club treasurer because of his guileful character."

2. "The budget for the party is limited, so please be lavish with your spending on decorations."

5. "The vote in favor of the new mascot was unanimous. It's great to see such dissension."

Skill: Antonyms

It's Okay to Be Contrary

Reproduce this page and cut the strips apart for an activity that will help students sharpen their skills with antonyms. One student draws a strip of paper from a hat or basket and reads it aloud to the group. The group (with the help of their dictionaries) must decide if the statement includes a pair of antonyms. If so, they give a "YES" answer to the example. Otherwise, they answer, "NO."

1. I'm not uncouth. I'm refined.

2. She called me a prodigy and an imbecile.

3. I can hardly stand to listen to your trumpet playing. It's so tinny and resonant.

4. Her goal is to expunge poverty. She wants to obliterate it, too.

5. He's smarmy. He's also unctuous.

6. Your clothes are immodest and decorous.

7. The FBI held a covert, clandestine meeting.

8. What a mediocre and spectacular poem!

9. My neighbor is domineering and subservient.

10. Your brother is impudent. Mine is timorous.

11. Don't impede our progress. Don't facilitate it either!

12. The fissures in the Earth's surface look a lot like crevasses.

Dynamic Duos

These dynamic duos are pairs of synonyms. Use them to launch a hunt for more synonyms and for some other words that express the opposite meaning of the duo. Have students give two additional synonyms and two antonyms for each pair.

1. vivid, bright

Synonyms: _____

_____

Antonyms: _____

_____

2. arduous, wearisome

Synonyms: _____

_____

Antonyms: _____

_____

3. mesmerize, bewitch

Synonyms: _____

_____

Antonyms: _____

_____

4. spurious, bogus

Synonyms: _____

_____

Antonyms: _____

_____

5. bravery, fortitude

Synonyms: _____

_____

Antonyms: _____

_____

6. obscure, indistinct

Synonyms: _____

_____

Antonyms: _____

_____

7. savory, toothsome

Synonyms: _____

_____

Antonyms: _____

_____

8. sagacious, shrewd

Synonyms: _____

_____

Antonyms: _____

_____

9. scuttle, skedaddle

Synonyms: _____

_____

Antonyms: _____

_____

A Trio of Clues

Each group of words below is a trio of clues that leads to an unknown word. Each threesome includes a synonym, an antonym, and a homonym for the mystery word. Write a trio of clues on the board. Students must examine each trio and think of ONE word that could be a synonym for one of them, an antonym for another one, and a homonym the other word.

1. bard, restricted, permitted

2. major, miner, insignificant

3. idol, employed, inactive

4. courage, medal, cowardice

5. lesson, diminish, increase

6. knead, luxury, necessity

7. tight, loose, taught

8. stationery, mobile, motionless

9. delightful, grizzly, frightful

10. shone, exhibited, hidden

Example:

proved, surmised, guest

Answer: guessed

It's a synonym for surmised.
It's an antonym for proved.
It's a homonym for guest.

The Missing Link

Give students these ten "before and after" word chains. Challenge them to find the missing links in ten minutes or less. The missing link can be used to turn each of the other words into a compound word, completing the second half of the first compound word, and the first half of the second compound word.

1.   note _____ keeper

2. peanut _____ fly

3.   foot _____ room

4.   over _____ out

5.   out _____ way

6.   birth _____ light

7.   quick _____ box

8.   high _____ side

9.   touch _____ stairs

10.   rain _____ tie

Example:

fire _____ walk =

fire **SIDE** walk

(fireside and sidewalk)

---

38   *Smart Starters* — Vocabulary

Copyright ©2005 by Incentive Publications, Inc., Nashville, TN.

Very Classy Words

Lots of words have *class*! These groups of words, in particular, are classy because all the words in each group fit into one *class*ification. Read the group of words to students or write them on the board. Ask students to examine them closely and identify a class to which all words in the group could belong.

Note: There may be more than one answer. The class may be a particular structural characteristic.

1. garish   plausible   diverse   hasty   marginal

2. monotonous   bilateral   decathlon   triune   quadruped

3. tempura   braise   fricassee   fondue   sauté

4. project   rejection   dejected   eject   trajectory

5. decrepit   dilapidated   rickety   battered   ramshackle

6. debark   predestined   encode   secluded   recapitulate

7. propriety   tact   gentility   decorum   dignity

8. narcosis   halitosis   paralysis   analysis   symbiosis

What's the Connection?

Give this list to students. Ask them to identify the relationship in all ten of the analogies. The last six are not complete. After identifying the relationship, students can suggest ways to complete them.

1. *Scream* is to *sound* as *caramel* is to *taste*.

2. *Warm* is to *scalding* as *cool* is to *freezing*.

3. *Peril* is to *danger* as *hectic* is to *chaotic*.

4. *Giraffe* is to *vertebrate* as *jellyfish* is to *invertebrate*.

5. *Sainthood* is to *saint* as *championship* is to _____.

6. *Surgeon* is to _____ as *detective* is to *investigate*.

7. *Linguini* is to pasta as *copper* is to _____.

8. *Disapprove* is to condone as *haughty* is to _____.

9. _____ is to mimic as *insolvent* is to penniless.

10. *Bothersome* is to *terrifying* as _____ is to *freezing*.

> An analogy consists of two pairs of words.
>
> The relationship between the words in one pair must be the same relationship as that between the words in the other pair.

Follow the Pattern

To solve these analogies, students will first need to find the relationship between the two words that are given. Then they can follow the pattern to complete the analogy with another pair of words.

> Note: palomino : horse :: emperor : penguin

This abbreviated way of writing an analogy is read: *Palomino* is to *horse* as *emperor* is to *penguin*.

1. prevent : forestall :: _____ : _____

2. schooner : ocean :: _____ : _____

3. physician : prescribe :: _____ : _____

4. unusual : bizarre :: _____ : _____

5. loathsome : loathe :: _____ : _____

6. inept : graceful :: _____ : _____

7. capillary : circulation :: _____ : _____

8. éclair : chefs :: _____ : _____

9. malleable : copper :: _____ : _____

10. forewarn : foreclose :: _____ : _____

The Heart of a Word

The heart of a word is its **root**, or base word part. The meaning of the root determines the core of meaning for a word. Prefixes, suffixes, and endings can add to the root meaning, but the word's final meaning is dependent upon the meaning of its root. Students should work together to identify the root part for each of these words and agree upon (or find) the meaning of the root.

1. cardiologist

2. cosmopolitan

3. abbreviate

4. centigrade

5. lucrative

6. manual

7. victorious

8. pendulum

9. pacifist

10. junction

11. applaud

12. capital

13. tripod

14. cryptogram

15. flamboyant

16. fraternity

17. luminous

18. mobility

From the Ground Up

Words grow out of their **roots**! Have students brush up on the meanings of root word parts with this quick exercise. They will polish root skills and stretch their thinking skills at the same time. The list below gives meanings for root words. Students should name the root, then find two words that are "grown" from that root!

1. to act

2. measure

3. sea

4. break

5. move

6. write

7. sound

8. empty

9. father

10. cut

11. sleep

12. sun

Example:
climb: *scend*
descend, ascension

Distinctive Beginnings

The chart contains some of the many distinctive beginnings that can be added to words. Give the chart to students and challenge them to write one or more words that begin with each prefix.

meaning	prefix	example words	meaning	prefix	example words
before	*ante* *fore* *pre*		not; without	*in* *an* *im*	
after	*post*		against	*anti* *contra*	
under	*sub* *subter*		out; outside of	*ex* *extra*	
around	*peri* *circum*		backwards	*retro*	
together	*co*		above	*super* *hyper*	

Puzzling over Prefixes

Use this quick oral exercise to practice the meanings of prefixes. Read each example to students and let them identify the prefix and guess its meaning. Check the dictionary if there is any doubt about the meanings.

1. collaborate	8. tetrahedron	15. combination
2. abstain	9. posterior	16. ultimate
3. omnipotent	10. synchronized	17. intravenous
4. contraindicator	11. paranormal	18. mesoderm
5. telepathic	12. superior	19. polytheism
6. excommunicate	13. circumnavigate	20. equidistant
7. millipede	14. anaerobic	21. semicircle

Suffix Circles

Use a stack of plain paper plates to brush up on the meanings and uses of suffixes. Give each student a paper plate and a suffix. Ask them to follow the simple instructions below in the time you have allotted for the activity (about 10 minutes).

1. Write the suffix in large print in the center of the plate.

2. Find the meaning of the suffix. Write it in small print beneath the suffix.

3. Find and write as many words as you can that have the suffix. Write the words as spokes on the wheel.

Some suffixes to use:

–ence	–ist	–fy	–ible	–able	–ile
–ive	–ic	–ous	–some	–like	–ly
–ism	–ize	–ary	–tion	–ment	–al
–hood	–hip	–ness	–ess	–ity	–ance
–ar	–er	–or	–ary	–ent	–ant

Meaningful Endings

The meaning of a word can change drastically with just the addition or change of a suffix. Help students stay sharp on the meanings of suffixes with this fast-paced practice. Students can work in small groups to race the clock and find words that match these meanings.

	word	meaning	word	meaning
1.	_____	like terror	_____	to cause to have terror
2.	_____	result of agreeing	_____	capable of agreeing
3.	_____	without a child	_____	like a child
4.	_____	one who does art	_____	showing skill and artistry
5.	_____	of the senses	_____	to make sensitive to
6.	_____	state of being red	_____	resembling red
7.	_____	resembling neighbors	_____	being a group of neighbors
8.	_____	acts of a hero	_____	act of being a hero
9.	_____	pertaining to music	_____	one who makes music
10.	_____	one who studies	_____	behaving like a student

Pass It On to Add On

Start with a root and add *affixes* (**prefixes** and **suffixes**) to create a word with a specific meaning.

Write each of these roots on an index card. Have students sit in a circle and give one root card to each person. Ask the group to follow these directions:

- Add a prefix to the root on your card.
- Pass the card to your right.
- Add a suffix to the word (or partial word) on this card to form a whole word.
- Pass the card to your right.
- Write the word's meaning on this card.

> *Example:*
>
> Start with a root word . . . . *fin*
> Add a prefix . . . . *infin*
> Add a suffix . . . . *infinite*
> Tell the meaning . . . . . . *without end,*
>   *or endless*

1. fer	7. loc	13. act	19. puls	25. pop
2. flam	8. mob	14. dic	20. vac	26. ten
3. celer	9. jec	15. norm	21. whole	27. sequ
4. mar	10. port	16. scend	22. lum	28. struct
5. define	11. son	17. junct	23. theo	29. tort
6. phon	12. derm	18. cep	24. verg	30. turb

Verbal Dissections

Dissection means the act of separating something into two parts. This exercise encourages students to dissect some words in order to get a clear picture of their meanings. Work together to read each word and separate it into two (or more) parts. Find the meaning of each part. This will help the group agree on the meaning of the whole world.

	the word	the parts	the meaning
Example:	**explode**	**ex (out) + plode (blow)**	**to blow out**

1. horrific

2. perimeter

3. removable

4. spherical

5. agonize

6. injection

7. telepathic

8. dermatologist

9. caustic

Short Cuts

These are abbreviations you need to know. They are short cuts to words. Nevertheless, they are used frequently enough that knowing them is important.

Gather students into groups of two or three. Give the list below to each group. Challenge them to find the meaning of at least 12 of the abbreviations. They should write a sentence of some kind demonstrating that they understand the abbreviation.

1. a.m.
2. anon.
3. apt.
4. assoc.
5. asst.
6. atty.
7. cal.

8. dept.
9. db
10. d.b.a.
11. etc.
12. e.g.
13. govt.
14. et al

15. ml
16. vs.
17. a.k.a.
18. blvd.
19. i.e.
20. r.p.m.
21. kg.

> *Example:*
> *Shirley B. Silver, a.k.a. Shifty Shirl, was arrested yesterday and charged with bank robbery.*

More Short Cuts

It's easy to take a short cut. Sometimes the short cut for a phrase or expression is more familiar than the words themselves. Back up and review the full meaning.

Assign an acronym to each student. Ask them to create a visual representation of the full phrase. This can be a picture, cartoon, or design of some sort. Each drawing should be labeled (on the back) and shared with the whole group so that other students can try to guess the acronym represented.

1. ASAP	7. DOA	13. IQ	19. SCUBA
2. CD	8. ESP	14. IRS	20. ICU
3. COD	9. RDA	15. POW	21. LASER
4. CPR	10. FBI	16. RN	22. RADAR
5. DA	11. AWOL	17. SASE	23. SONAR
6. FAQs	12. DVD	18. www	24. ZIP (Code)

What's the Word?

What is the one word that works to make a compound word out of each of the other words in the group? This will take sharp thinking!

Give the list to small groups, set the timer for ten minutes, and see how many of the mystery words can be found. (The missing word might be the first word in the compound, or it might be the final word in the compound.)

1. ___*(stand)*___ off, band, grand, by

2. _____ shell, weed, shore, sick

3. _____ touch, sun, town, stairs

4. _____ glow, book, hole, inch

5. _____ set, back, town, line

6. _____ fire, walk, out, ways

7. _____ friend, shape, wreck, owner

8. _____ board, way, side, about

9. _____ water, out, night, back

10. _____ look, doors, standing, rage

Words to "Note"-ice

Once students track down the meanings of these musical terms, they'll be able to listen to music with more appreciation and curiosity. Work as a group to define each musical term. Then play a selection of music and ask students to listen for the various musical "events" or approaches. When time permits, listen to other pieces of music, trying out different kinds.

1. arpeggio	5. piano	9. crescendo	13. intermezzo
2. adagio	6. capriccio	10. falsetto	14. staccato
3. bravura	7. sonata	11. forte	15. vivace
4. concerto	8. legato	12. fortissimo	16. a cappella

Don't Be Intimidated!

Big words can be intimidating, but only until you know what they mean. Help students escape the fear of big words with this painless exercise. Give one big word to each group of 2-3 students. Their job is to find the meaning and create a sentence using the phrase provided with the word.

1. **pontification**
   waving his arms wildly

2. **misappropriation**
   slinked away into the night

3. **circumlocution**
   left the class entirely confused

4. **extemporaneous**
   how to get rid of lice

5. **heterogeneous**
   interesting group of friends

6. **juxtaposition**
   teenagers and octogenarians

7. **noctambulist**
   dangerously close to the cliff

8. **perambulation**
   lost at the county fair

9. **pusillanimous**
   danger to the whole mission

10. **versimilitude**
    waving his arms wildly

11. **dissemination**
    plenty of shady ideas

12. **subcutaneous**
    a trip to the emergency room

Phrases with Flair

They've got style! They've got flair! They're oh, so much fun to roll off your tongue! But what do they mean? These phrases, borrowed from other languages, are frequently used by English-speaking people. Ask students to find the meaning of each phrase and think about a situation in which it might be used. The list might be split up among 5 or 6 small groups.

1. a la carte

2. faux pas

3. ad hoc

4. ipso facto

5. cordon bleu

6. avant garde

7. par excellence

8. nom de plum

9. ipso facto

10. coup de grace

11. non sequitur

12. cul – de – sac

13. laissez faire

14. magnum opus

15. ad nauseam

16. fait accompli

17. tête-à-tête

18. nouveau riche

If there is time, finish the lesson by asking each
student or group of students to think of a *non sequitur.*

Borrowed Words

The English language is enhanced by thousand of wonderful words borrowed from other languages. These are just a few of them. Students can have fun learning their meanings and meeting the challenge of communicating those meanings to the whole class.

Give each word to a pair of students. Their job is to find its correct pronunciation and meaning, and then to decide a way to demonstrate the meaning to other students. Drawings are banned—students must *show* the meaning.

1. bourgeois	*6. repartee*	*11. élan*
2. coiffure	*7. malaise*	*12. impasse*
3. gauche	*8. julienne*	*13. mélange*
4. soupcon	*9. blasé*	*14. alto*
5. vignette	*10. détente*	*15. ingénue*

Curious Contradictions

Read these examples to students. Let them identify the contradiction in each one.

> An ***oxymoron*** is an expression, phrase, or sentence that contains contradictions. One word or idea seems to contradict or nullify another word or idea.

Examples:

1. terribly happy
2. good gossip
3. deafening silence
4. modern history
5. awfully pleased
6. old news
7. black light

8. bittersweet
9. small crowd
10. sanitary landfill
11. alone together
12. definite maybe
13. minor crisis
14. unbiased opinion

15. ill health
16. The more things change, the more they stay the same.
17. I am deeply superficial
18. I'd give my right arm to be ambidextrous.

Words That Wow!

Palindromes are words, phrases or sentences that read the same forward and backwards. Work with students to collect as many of them as you can in five minutes.

Then give these beginnings of phrases to students. Ask them to finish them in a way that will create a palindrome.

Example: **rats (add rat backwards) = rat star**

Examples:	
level	mom
pop	madam
noon	sis
Bob	toot
eve	SOS
noon	did
kayak	dud
dad	deed

1. tops _____

2. lion _____

3. No lemons _____

4. a santa _____

5. party_____

6. Was it a b_____

7. Ana, nab a _____

8. Del saw _____

9. Step on _____

10. Do geese_____

11. Wonton? _____

12. straw _____

Right Place, Wrong Word

Read these sentences aloud. Ask students to listen for the malapropisms and give the correct word(s).

> A **malapropism** is an accidental or ludicrous misuse of a word, caused by confusing it with a similar word.

1. I broke my right arm and learned to write with my left hand, so now I'm **amphibious**.

2. Hey Jamie! Try some of these great garlic-flavored **neutrons** on your salad!

3. Mom, I started a fire in the kitchen. But don't worry, I put it out with the fire **distinguisher**.

4. My older sister is looking for an **illegible** bachelor.

5. Life was terribly hard for the **pheasants** in the Middle Ages.

6. The climate of the Sahara Desert is so dry that you need **irritation** to grow anything.

7. We just finished an amazing yacht trip that included **cursing** on the Caribbean Sea for a week.

8. *Don't, she'd, wasn't, they'll, you're,* and *it's* are all **contraptions**.

9. The violin player is extremely successful. She's at the **pineapple** of her career.

10. My favorite dinosaurs are the **thesaurus** and the **bronchitis**.

More Malapropisms

It's a challenge to identify a malapropism when you hear one. It's an even greater challenge to create one! Give the following pairs of words to students. Let them work for several minutes to create a malapropism that misuses one of these words in place of the other in the pair.

1. abominable – abdominal

2. comma – comet

3. historical – hysterical

4. matrimony – acrimony

5. alteration – altercation

6. papooses – porpoises

7. turbans – turbines

8. tranquility – hostility

9. origin – organ

10. cordon – accordion

11. evacuate – evaporate

12. vinegarette – vignette

Weird (but Real) Words

Words such as sillabub or quidnunc sound really strange, but that doesn't mean they aren't real words! Provide good dictionaries and let students work in pairs to find the weird words in these questions. Once they know the definitions, they'll be able to answer the questions.

1. Is it possible that a ***sillabub*** could be ***esculent***?

2. Which would you choose: two hours of ***skullduggery***, or a day keeping watch over a ***smatchet***?

3. Would you leave your beloved cat with a family that promises to ***fustigate*** her daily?

4. Which would be a more suitable place for a competitive swimmer to practice: a ***natatorium*** or a ***gerontocomium***?

5. Which would you prefer to have as a friend: a ***pugilist*** or a ***quidnunc***?

Write a question that someone could answer after they find the meanings of these two words: ***avuncular*** and ***dyspepsia***.

Name Two

Work together as a group or class to meet this challenge. Name two things (or people, or places) that fit each description. Brainstorm ideas and keep the best two for each one.

Name two . . .

1. good names for a *flibbertigibbet*   _____   _____

2. accomplishments that deserve *kudos*   _____   _____

3. things you might feed to an *affenpinscher*   _____   _____

4. ways that a *coccyx* might become injured   _____   _____

5. questions to ask a *funambulist*   _____   _____

6. ingredients found in *jambalaya*   _____   _____

7. places a *discalsed* boy should not go   _____   _____

8. things you could *thwack* without getting into trouble   _____   _____

9. situations in which you have been *nonplussed*   _____   _____

10. things that might be *unctuous*   _____   _____

Vowels Galore

Some words are blessed with a plethora of vowels! These words are fun to read, write, and say. Give copies of this page to students. Challenge them to find more words with multiple vowels.

Abracadabra has 5 **a**'s.

Catamaran has 4 **a**'s.

Write 3 words with 3 or more **a**'s.

Defenselessness has 5 **e**'s.

Beekeeper has 5 **e**'s.

Write 3 words with 3 or 4 **e**'s.

Indivisibility has 6 **i**'s.

Insignificant has 4 **i**'s.

Write 3 words with 3 or more **i**'s.

Cumulous has 3 **u**'s.

Unscrupulous has 4 **u**'s.

Write 3 words with 2 or more **u**'s.

Cookbook has 4 **o**'s.

Locomotion has 4 **o**'s.

Write 3 words with 3 or more **o**'s.

Body Talk

Read the body talk to students. Let them take turns responding to each quotation with a statement which shows that they understand what the term means.

Example:

> *The doctor is worried about that **aneurysm**.*

> *Yes, that dangerous, bulging blood vessel could burst at any moment.*

1. The doctor is worried about the **aneurysm**.
2. Her cancer has **metastasized**.
3. I'm **hemorrhaging**!
4. Bob suffers from **gastroenteritis**.
5. Joe has an infection in his **pericardium**.
6. She's had **arteriosclerosis** for years.
7. After the accident, Tom developed a **hematoma**.
8. Dan just had an attack of **hypoglycemia**.
9. I picked up **hepatitis** on my jungle cruise.
10. Stay away from **carcinogenic** substances.
11. She's cleaning the **toxins** out of her body.
12. We're glad that the tumor is **benign**.
13. Dr. Arch is my **podiatrist**.
14. I'm scheduled for an **encephalogram** today.
15. What were the results of your **biopsy**?

Extraordinary Expressions

Has anyone ever asked you to hold your horses? What were they thinking? Maybe you don't even own any horses! The language is full of these extraordinary phrases that do not say exactly what they mean. Help students become familiar with some of the idioms and figures of speech that may be unfamiliar to them. Model a good explanation. Assign a figure of speech to each student with the following directions:

1. Draw a picture that shows the literal meaning of the expression.

2. Take the expression home, carry it around, share it with others, and find out what it means.

3. Come back to school with an explanation of what the expression really means.

Her boss is throwing him to the wolves.	The family is glad to be in the red.
Keep your nose to the grindstone.	It was the straw that broke the camel's back.
She's just casting pearls before swine.	Don't get all bent out of shape.
You're barking up the wrong tree.	Ginny bit off more than she could chew.
If I had my druthers, I'd go home.	Don't air your dirty linen in public.
Every dog has his day.	Get busy and bring home the bacon.
That's just adding insult to injury.	She's jumped out of the frying pan and into the fire.
She's at the end of her rope.	He studied for the test at the eleventh hour.
They were armed to the teeth.	Get off your high horse

Captivating Collections

A troop of Girl Scouts, a squadron of soldiers, and a gaggle of geese all have something in common. Each phrase uses a collective noun to name its group. Students can build familiarity with some interesting collective nouns by asking them to match the two lists of words below. Have them work in small groups and get help from their dictionaries.

Group A			Group B		
1. bevy	9. sleuth	17. murder	bears	kangaroos	beavers
2. colony	10. bask	18. skulk	foxes	leopards	dolphins
3. fleet	11. scourge	19. belt	angels	baboons	coyotes
4. leap	12. pack	20. pod	camels	aircraft	asteroids
5. army	13. troop	21. pride	caterpillars	mosquitoes	crows
6. bed	14. quiver	22. brood	peacocks	bats	whales
7. host	15. lodge	23. congress	arrows	crocodiles	hens
8. school	16. kindle	24. caravan	kittens	swans	clams

A Mathematical Cipher

A cipher is a code—a secret way to communicate. There are all kinds of ciphers. This one "disguises" the words by using letters of the alphabet to substitute for each other.

Give students a copy of the cipher below. Each letter of the alphabet stands for a different letter of the alphabet. Use the three clues to break the code and figure out what the message says. (The answer is a funny question about math!)

Clues

F = L

J = E

O = F

N O	L	B N B J Y S	P J A W J J
— —	—	— — — — — —	— — — — — —

L B A I J	N G	W N A R Y ,	L W J	L F F
— — — — —	— —	— — — — — ,	— — —	— — —

C Y R J W	L B A F J G	D W C B A ? ?
— — — — —	— — — — — —	— — — — — ? ?

A Cipher from the Past

Here's a cipher to crack. Use what you know about history to help you solve the code. The question is a pun about a famous American.

Each letter stands for a different letter. For instance, every time you see an *O*, it really means *S*.

Clues

O	=	S
V	=	R
N	=	E

R G R   I N Y O T   V S O O ' O
— — —   — — — — —   — — — — ' —

J V G N X R O   M C D D   W N V   E G O O
— — — — — — —   — — — —   — — —   — — — —

O N F – C X R – O N F ?
— — — – — — — – — — — ?

Skill: Word Associations

The Right One

Sharpen word skills *and* thinking skills with this clever game. The idea is to find one word that can be paired with all the words in each group. The "answer" word might be put in front of or after each of the other words. The two words together form a compound word or just a familiar expression. Challenge teams of students to find all the answers in ten minutes or less.

1. roar	stairs	set	seven	
2. swatter	horse	gad	ball	
3. bill	walk	score	room	
4. string	pole	bag	kidney	
5. cake	cottage	cloth	blue	
6. goose	first	town	stairs	
7. shape	mate	friend	member	

8. gold	pan	storm	mop
9. post	Golden	keeper	way
10. hum	ear	corps	beat
11. nail	green	tack	Tom
12. nip	tom	copy	walk
13. stone	harvest	struck	blue
14. fall	white	logged	high

Alphabet Advice

Alphabet Advice uses words starting with sequential letters of the alphabet. Students can work in small groups to see how far they can get through the alphabet in the available time.

Ask students to compose a 26-word collection of good advice. They start with the letter *A* and continue with words that begin with each successive letter in the alphabet.

Example:

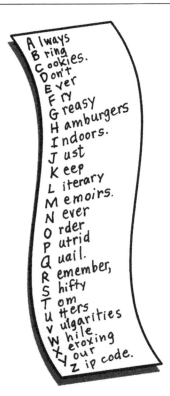

A lways
B ring
C ookies.
D on't
E ver
F ry
G reasy
H amburgers
I ndoors.
J ust
K eep
L iterary
M emoirs.
N ever
O rder
P utrid
Q uail.
R emember,
S hifty
T om
U tters
V ulgarities
W hile
X eroxing
Y our
Z ip code.

Acrostic Antics

> An ***acrostic*** is a poem or puzzle in which the first letters of each line (when read in order) spell a word or phrase. The lines in an acrostic may be one word, a phrase, or a whole sentence.

Share some acrostics with students. Ask them to try creating an acrostic using a favorite word or name. Suggest that they build the acrostic as a riddle with all the lines giving clues about the characteristics of something or the meaning of a word.

Examples:

Jet-like force pushes away

Everything near the explosion site,

Tossed scraps of rock and metal

Thrown hundreds of feet

Into the clear night air.

Silence shattered,

Objects scattered,

Nothing left but scattered rubble.

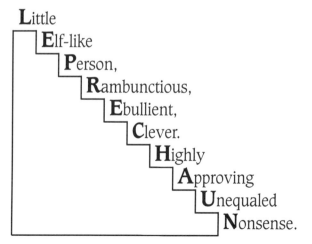

Little
Elf-like
Person,
Rambunctious,
Ebullient,
Clever.
Highly
Approving
Unequaled
Nonsense.

Reversals & Rearrangements

An **anagram** is a word that can become a different word when the letters are reversed or rearranged. Anagrams can be also be phrases or sentences.

Share some anagrams with students. Let them try their hands at changing the words below into words that match the descriptions given. If time permits, encourage them to make up several anagrams of their own!

Word	Change To Word Which Means . . .		Word	Change To Word Which Means . . .
1. STARE	rips		7. SUPERSONIC	section in an orchestra
2. HAPPIEST	writings found on tombstones		8. RENTALS	horns on some animals
3. PAROLED	large cat with spots		9. RECITAL	can be found in a newspaper
4. TAXES	U.S.'s biggest state		10. WOLVES	some letters in the alphabet
5. SLIMES	grins		11. SCHOOLMASTER	where he or she might be found
6. VEERS	cut			

Examples:	*TEA — EAT*	*SMART — TRAMS*
	BRAD — DRAB	*TWELVE + ONE — ELEVEN + TWO*

A Shook Crook & a Lone Stone

A *hink pink* is a rhyming pair of one-syllable words that includes an adjective and a noun. A *nervous burglar* is a *shook crook* and a *solitary rock* is a *lone stone*. A hinky-pinky is a rhyming pair of two-syllable words, and a hinkity-pinkity is a rhyming pair of three-syllable words.

Read these clues to students and enjoy the game of figuring out the rhyming pairs from the clues. Encourage students to add additional adjective-noun rhyming pairs to the list. They'll need to create the clues so others can figure out what the words are.

Hink-Pinks:

1. wasp's patellas
2. antique rocker
3. noisy mob
4. not-quite-right tune
5. flippant lie

Hinky-Pinkies:

6. center violin
7. faster parson
8. romantic stove
9. broader arachnid
10. dill five-cent piece
11. different mom
12. drabber hue
13. professors' grandstands
14. calm guy
15. more knowledgeable penny-pincher

Hinkity-Pinkities:

16. non-chocolate ape
17. evil preacher
18. political leader's home

Purveyors of Pun

> A ***pun*** is a play on words—a statement that uses words or combinations of words to create a joke.

Puns are often used to create names which describe certain people. These signs advertise businesses for interesting characters. Share them with students. Encourage the students to make their own signs for one or more of the occupations below.

seamstress	dentist
sausage maker	chimney cleaner
undertaker	pastry chef
brain surgeon	lumberjack
drummer	sailor
trampolinist	firefighter
veterinarian	candle maker
seamstress	saxophone player
garbage collector	kindergarten teacher

Dr. Yul C. Kleerly
Optometry

LOTTA SPRAY
Licensed
Beautician

PROFESSOR
MOE KWIZZES
HISTORY

Mac A. Deal
Car Salesman

Hope Utipp
Waitress
20 years experience

Ima C.
deMoon
Astronaut

Holden Yernose
Certified Dive Instructor

Rebus Puzzlers

A ***rebus*** is a puzzle or coded message that presents an idea visually. The way words, letters, or pictures are displayed gives a clue to what is meant. To figure out the meaning, students need to study each image carefully and try to see it in a way that is different from the obvious.

Share these rebus puzzles with students. Give them 10 minutes to figure out what phrase or idea is represented by the eight examples.

1.
M   E
L   A

2. ✂ LOOSE

4. HA IRS

3. read

5. F I R E / F I R E

6. Lang**4**uage

7. arrest / YOU'RE

8. TIME abdefg

More Rebus Puzzlers

Share these rebus puzzles with students. Give them 10 minutes to figure out what phrase or idea is represented by the examples. When they've "cracked" them all, ask them to choose one of the phrases at the bottom of the page and to create an original rebus.

1. **1 1 1 1 1**s
   4:15 pm

2. 13579 **RU**

3. settle ↓

4. **rosie**

5. ca JUST se

6. h e a d heels

7. **time time**

8. wear **LONG**

---

split pea • ahead of his time • out on a limb • thinking outside the box • lost in space

Proverbs Revisited

Proverbs are such a familiar part of the language that most of us don't stop to pay attention to them. Review a few of the most familiar (such as *"A bird in the hand is worth two in the bush,"* or *"Don't count your chickens before they're hatched."*). Talk about what the proverbs mean. Give students a chance to think about how they would finish each of these proverbs to make them into wise sayings. Enjoy sharing the results.

1. _____ and _____ smell in three days.

2. As you make your bed, you must _____.

3. Better the devil you know than _____.

4. Nothing is certain except _____ and _____

5. There is no _____ among thieves.

6. People who live in glass houses _____.

7. Every family has a ____ in the closet.

8. All roads lead to _____.

9. Blood is thicker than _____.

10. Don't cut off your nose to _____.

11. Fight fire with _____.

12. Good _____ make good neighbors.

13. They that dance must _____.

14. _____ makes a weak man wise.

Good Neighbors

The object of this game is to find a pair of words that match the definitions and are dictionary neighbors. This means they are found in a dictionary very close to each other.

	Word 1:	*Word 2*
1.	deadly, damaging	sluggish, apathetic
2.	to block or impede	to thrust out or to interfere
3.	to watch secretly	a young pigeon
4.	a woodwind instrument	a medieval trumpet
5.	crazy	a type of fish
6.	a wailing ghost	breed of small chicken

> If time permits, ask students to work in pairs to add more items to this game.

Chew Your Doors!

A ***spoonerism*** is way of playing with words that switches the beginning sounds of two words within a phrase or sentence. They are named after an English clergyman, William Archibald Spooner, who suffered from poor eyesight. One of his famous original confused statements was this: "For real excitement, give me a well-boiled icicle." *(well-oiled bicycle)*

Share these examples with students. Give them a few seconds to decipher each mix-up. If time permits, students can write some of their own.

1. *Pardon me, ma'am, but your ship is slowing.*
2. *Let's get to the shawl and do some mopping.*
3. *Did you bring the snail tracks for the hike?*
4. *Oh, no! Your news is a blushing crow!*
5. *Tom, did you chew your doors?*
6. *Your story is a lack of pies!*
7. *Watch out for rumbling tocks.*
8. *Some thinkle peep I am not smoo tart.*

Tom Swifties

A ***Tom Swiftie*** is a sophisticated play on words. Each Tom Swiftie begins with a quotation (attributed to Tom) and ends with a pun.

Share some of these examples with students. Let them identify the puns. Then give them some time to try writing a few Tom Swifties on their own.

"The storm knocked out my electricity," Tom said darkly.

"You need a shave," Tom said sharply.

"I'm sorry that your aunt died," Tom said gravely.

"I've just left the dentist's office," Tom said numbly.

"Please sharpen the pencils," Tom said pointedly.

"This steak is not well cooked," Tom rarely said.

"Are you studying opera?" Tom asked melodically.

"Watch out for the dynamite!" Tom said explosively.

"I love Chinese food." Tom said wantonly.

"Finish scouring the sink," Tom ordered abrasively.

Sometimes the pun is in the verb, adjective or preposition.

"I need a plumber!" Tom piped up.

"I see you have a pet goat," Tom kidded.

"I love the green carpet in your office," Tom said in a colorful tone.

"I'm sure the defendant is guilty," Tom said with conviction.

"Yes, I felt the earthquake," Tom said, with cracks in his voice.

What a Conundrum!

> A **conundrum** is a sticky problem or question.
> Often the solution to a conundrum involves a pun.

It's always a challenge to solve a conundrum. Besides that, it's just plain fun. Give students ten minutes to try to solve these. Provide the clues to help with the answers or let students find answers without the clues. Remind them that the answer involves a clever play on words. Ask students to try to create a conundrum of their own (with a pun in the answer).

1. Why did the baby chick get thrown out of math class?
   Clue: *for _____ during a test.*

2. Why couldn't the pony talk?
   Clue: *because he was a little _____.*

3. Why are birds grouchy in the morning?
   Clue: *because their _____ are over dew.*

4. What kind of haircuts do sea captains prefer?
   Clue: *anything _____.*

5. Why don't monkeys in the jungle play cards anymore?
   Clue: *because there are just too many _____.*

6. What happened to the frog's car when his parking meter expired?
   Clue: *It got _____.*

Glossary

a la carte – from the menu, priced separately

abrasive – harsh

acrid – harsh tasting or smelling

acrimonious – bitter, nasty

ad hoc – for a specific, limited purpose

ad nauseam – to a ridiculous degree

adroit – skilled

affenpinscher – dog breed

affiliated – connected with

agitate – stir up

alleviate – to ease or relieve

alleviated – lessened

allude – refer to

alto – low female voice

ambidextrous – able to use either hand

ample – plenty

aquatic – relating to water

arduous – difficult

avant garde – ahead of the times, in the forefront

bard – a poet-singer

barred – blocked

beguile – fascinate

beleaguered – besieged

belligerent – hostile

benevolent – kind

bequeath – leave in a will or hand down

bewitch – to charm

blithe – cheerful

bogus – phony

bonanza – sudden profit

bourgeois – middle class

bravery – fearlessness

bright – shining or brilliant

brouhaha – uproar

burl – clod

cache – stockpile

cantankerous – cranky

chafe – irritate

chastisement – punishment

churlish – grumpy

circular – round

circumlocution – talking in circles

clandestine – secret

coccyx – tail bone

coiffure – hairstyle

commodious – roomy

conscientious – responsible,

contentious – argumentative, quarrelsome

convivial – jolly

copious – abundant

cordon bleu – blue ribbon

coup de grace – stroke of mercy, last straw, or final blow

covert – secret

cowardice – lack of courage

credible – believable
credulous – gullible
crepe – a type of crinkled fabric or paper
cul-de-sac – a street closed at one end
cunning – sly, shrewd
dank – damp, chilly
decorous – dignified, proper
decorum – politeness, tact
decrepit – broken-down
delightful – enjoyable, charming
demure – shy or modest
depreciate – lower the value
derelict – careless
deride – mock
derisive – scornful
desolate – sad
détente – relaxing of tensions
diffuse – spread out, scattered
dilapidated – rickety
diminish – reduce
discalsed – barefoot
disconsolate – depressed
disdainful – scornful
disparage – discredit, belittle

dissemination – to scatter far and wide
dissension – disagreement
docile – obedient, willing
domineering – bossy
dour – gloomy, unfriendly
dupe – trick
dynamic – energetic, forceful
effete – unproductive, worn out
eject – to drive out
élan – flair
elicit – to obtain information
elude – avoid, escape
elude – to escape
employed – in use, having a job
emprise – an undertaking
enigmatic – complicated
enthrall – spellbind
erratic – unpredictable
erudite – scholarly
eschew – give up, avoid
esculent – fit to be eaten
esteem – honor
exhibited – showed, revealed
exorbitant – excessive

expedient – helpful
expunge – get rid of
extemporaneous – not premeditated, unplanned
facilitate – make easier, assist the progress of
fait accompli – accomplished deed or feat
fastidious – choosy or fussy
fauna – animal life
faux pas – false step (socially embarrassing)
finesse – delicacy, tact
finicky – picky
fissures – cracks
flair – talent, aptitude
flibbertigibbet – a silly, flighty person
flogging – whipping or beating
fortitude – endurance
frenetic – frantic
frightful – scary, horrible
funambulist – tightrope walker
furtive – sneaky
fustigate – to beat with a stick

Glossary

gauche – clumsy, inept

gentility – politeness, elegance

gerontocomium – an institution that cares for elderly people

giddy – dizzy, light-headed

glide – soar, move smoothly

glower – scowl

gossamer – light, filmy

gregarious – friendly

grisly – gruesome, ghastly

grizzly – type of bear

grovel – cower or cringe

gruesome – horrible, hideous

guileful – deceitful

heterogeneous – of different origins

humdrum – dull

idle – inactive, at rest

idol – popular hero or godlike figure

illicit – illegal

illuminated – lit up

illusory – unreal, false

imbecile – a fool

impasse – deadlock

impasse – dilemma

impede – to slow or stop

impudent – rude

inactive – idle, unused

inane – silly

incite – provoke, urge on

incompetent – lacking ability

increase – make greater

indistinct – unclear, out of focus

inexplicable – unexplainable

infinitesimal – tiny, microscopic

ingénue – a naïve young woman

inopportune – inconvenient, awkward

inquisitive – curious

insidious – sly, deceitful

insignificant – unimportant

insolent – disrespectful

insouciant – carefree

interloper – outsider

inundate – flood, overflow

invective – harsh words

ipso facto – by the very fact

irascible – angry, irritable

irate – angry

jambalaya – a rice and meat dish

jocose – jolly

jocund – merry or jolly

jostle – push or shove

julienne – cut in long, thin strips

juxtaposition – to put side by side

knead – to work and shape with the hands

kudos – praise

laconic – short and to the point

laissez faire – hands off

largess – generosity

laud – praise

lavish – extravagant

legato – music with smooth sound

lessen – decrease

lesson – instruction

liege – loyal, faithful

listless – sluggish, lazy

loathe – hate

loose – unfastened, free

loquacious – talkative

lout – clod, dunce

lucrative – producing wealth

luminous – emitting light

luxury – extreme comfort, riches
macabre – horrible, gruesome
magnum opus – masterpiece
major – greater, foremost
malaise – vague feeling of illness
malice – ill will, evil intent
malleable – able to be bent
mariner – seaman, sailor
martinet – a hard master or tyrant
matinee – an afternoon performance
meager – skimpy, inadequate
medal – an honor, prize
mélange – mixture
memento – souvenir, keepsake
mesmerize – put in a trance
mesmerized – spellbound
mettle – courage, enthusiasm
mettlesome – spirited
minimize – to reduce or underestimate
minor – small, insignificant
misappropriation – to get in a bad or
    dishonest way
mobile – moveable
mollify – to calm down or soothe

momentous – important
moniker – nickname
motionless – still, unmoving
mottled – speckled
mythic – legendary or imaginary
natatorium – an indoor swimming
    pool
necessity – something needed
nefarious – wicked
noctambulist – one who walks in
    his/her sleep
nom de plum – pen name
    (pseudonym)
non sequitur – an illogical statement
    that doesn't follow from what was
    previously said
nonplussed – speechless, bewildered
notorious – famous
nouveau riche – suddenly wealthy
obliterate – wipe out
obscure – unclear, or to hide
ocelot – a medium-sized striped and
    spotted wildcat
onus – burden, blame

ooze – flow out slowly
ornate – fancy
outage – an interruption in electrical
    power
outface – to stare down
outflank – to get around
outlay – spending or cost
outlier – something that is situated
    away from the center
outmoded – out of style
outrageous – extreme, enormous
pacify – calm
palpitate – tremble
paltry – insignificant
par excellence – the height of
    excellence of something
paradox – a statement or idea that is
    contrary to what is expected
paraphernalia – equipment or gear
parity – equality
parsimonious – miserly
parsimony – stinginess
paunch – potbelly
peccadillo – slight fault

Glossary

penurious – stingy

perambulation – walking through, over, and around

pernicious – deadly, wicked

persnickety – fussy about small details

pertussis – whooping cough

piebald – spotted

piquant – spicy

plethora – excess

plummet – fall, plunge

pontification – speaking or acting in a pompous way

porous – honeycombed, spongy

pragmatic – practical

precipice – brink, a steep, overhanging place

precipitant – rash, impulsive

precipitous – extremely steep

prodigy – young genius

proliferate – increase rapidly

prolific – very productive

propriety – dignity, good manners

puce – dark red

pugilist – boxer

pugnacious – combative; belligerent, quarrelsome

pullet – young hen

punctilious – careful, precise about details

pungent – spicy

pusillanimous – cowardly

quadrangle – a four-sided enclosure

quadrant – an instrument for measuring altitude; an arc of 90°

quagmire – soft, muddy ground

quarry – something that is hunted, or a place where stone is mined

quartet – a group of four

quatrain – a group of four lines of verse

quay – a dock or pier

quell – quiet

queue – a waiting line, or a braid of hair

quibble – raise petty objections

quidnunc – a gossip

quiescent – at rest

rabble – mob

ramshackle – broken down, disorganized

rancor – hostility, hate

ravage – to devastate

ravish – to take away by force

rebuke – scold

recline – lie down

refined – polite and mannerly

reflect – to mirror or imitate

rend – tear; rip

repartee – a swift, witty reply

repast – a meal

reproof – scolding, criticism

repugnant – disgusting

resonant – full, rich

restricted – limited, confined by rules

sagacious – wise

salubrious – healthy

sanguine – cheerful

savory – tasty

schematic – a diagram

scrupulous – honest; precise

scuttle – scamper; move quickly

serpentine – twisting

serrated – notched on the edge

shone – past tense of shine

shown – came into view

shrewd – sly, tricky

sillabub – an 18th century creamy
   English dessert

skedaddle – hurry

skullduggery – dirty work

sleuth – detective

slither – move with a side-to-side
   motion

smarmy – insincere, slippery

smatchet – a small, nasty person
   (often a child)

soffit – the underside of a roof
   overhang

soupcon – a trace or suspicion of
   something

spritz – to spray

spurious – fake

squander – waste

staccato – disjointed, choppy music

stalemate – deadlock

stationery – writing paper

stodgy – stuffy, dull

stride – to walk with long steps

subcutaneous – beneath the skin

submissive – obedient, meek

subservient – excessively submissive

subtle – understated, indirect

sumptuous – luxurious

sweltering – hot

tact – discretion, diplomacy

taught – instructed

taut – tight

temperate – moderate

tenacious – stubborn; clinging

tête-à-tête – intimate meeting

thwack – thump, smack

tight – firm or stretched

timorous – timidness

tirade – long, denouncing speech

toothsome – attractive; delicious

torpor – sluggishness

tortuous – winding and twisting

torturous – very painful

treacle – molasses; syrup

trivial – unimportant

trudge – walk wearily

ubiquitous – seeming to be present
   everywhere

uncouth – boorish, rude

unctuous – smug, slippery

undulate – move in waves

unkempt – messy

unscrupulous – lacking principles

upbraid – scold

urbane – elegant, suave

vacillate – fluctuate

vacuous – silly

vapid – lacking flavor; dull

veer – swerve

verisimilitude – appearing to be true

vex – irritate

vignette – a sketch or scene

viscous – thick and sticky

vivid – bright and colorful

voracious – ravenous

wearisome – tiresome

weave – entwine: twist and turn

wholesome – healthy

whorl – spiral or coil

Answers

PAGE 9

Answers will vary.

PAGE 10

See glossary for word meanings. Answers may vary.

1. yes
2. pertussis
3. no
4. punctilious

PAGE 11

Answers will vary.

PAGE 12

See glossary for word meanings.

1. laconic
2. lauded
3. repast

4. commodious
5. sumptuous
6. temperate
7. adroit
8. scrupulous

PAGE 13

See glossary for word meanings. Answers will vary.

PAGE 14

See glossary for word meanings. Incorrect words are:

1. memento
2. porous
3. bequeath
4. parsimony
5. eschew
6. largess
7. quiescent

PAGE 15

See glossary for word meanings.

PAGE 16

See glossary for word meanings.

PAGE 17

See glossary for word meanings.

PAGE 18

See glossary for word meanings.

PAGE 19

1. momentous – adjective
   trivial – adjective
   reproof – noun
   elude – verb
   mariner – noun
2. momentous, trivial
3. Answers will vary.

4. Answers will vary.
5. All words have an affix (prefix or suffix).

PAGE 20

Answers will vary. See glossary for word meanings.

PAGE 21

Answers will vary. See glossary for word meanings.

PAGE 22

Answers will vary.

PAGE 23

Drawings will vary.

PAGE 24

Answers will vary. Check to see that presentations show at least three different meanings of the word.

PAGE 25

19 uses in the story: got up, stirring up, upset, up in arms, dressed up, makeup, set up, think up, climbed up, opened up, caught up, took up, closed up, got up, cleaned up, worked up, up to, stood up, what's up

Other uses: Answers will vary.

PAGE 26

Answers may vary somewhat.

1. terse – short, concise
2. beguiled – deceived
3. imminent – about to occur
4. feigned – pretended

PAGE 27

1. elude
2. credulous
3. illicit
4. precipitant
5. ravage
6. legato
7. tortuous
8. nefarious

PAGE 28

1. benevolent
2. lucrative
3. tirade
4. acrimonious
5. alleviated
6. ubiquitous

PAGE 29

1. tornado
2. villain
3. dark
4. sick
5. laugh
6. Martian

7. capture
8. ice cream cone

PAGE 30

Matching pairs:

1–25
2–16
3–13
4–17
5–23
6–28
7–18
8–20
9–21
10–24
11–22
12–27
14–29
15–26
19–30

PAGE 31

1. troublesome
2. placid

3. voracious
4. flair
5. finicky
6. insouciant
7. emprise
8. tease
9. quibble
10. vapid

PAGE 32

Answers will vary. See glossary for word meanings.

PAGE 33

Matches:

1–12
2–10
3–16
4–18
5–17
6–20
7–14
8–9

11–15
13–19

PAGE 34

Answers will vary. Some possibilities:

1. enigmatic – easy
2. chastisement – forgiveness
2. lavish – frugal
3. guileful – reliable
4. terminate – begin
5. dissension – agreement

PAGE 35

1. yes
2. yes
3. yes
4. no
5. no
6. yes
7. no
8. yes
9. yes

Answers

10. yes
11. yes
12. no

PAGE 36

Answers will vary.

PAGE 37

1. barred
2. minor
3. idle
4. mettle
5. lessen
6. need
7. taut
8. stationary
9. grisly
10. shown

PAGE 38

1. book
2. butter
3. ball
4. look
5. run
6. day

7. sand
8. way
9. down
10. bow

PAGE 39

Answers may vary.
Some possibilities:

1. all adjectives
2. all have prefixes that are related to numbers
3. food-related; foreign words
4. same root (ject)
5. similar meaning
6. all have prefixes
7. similar meaning
8. similar structure

PAGE 40

Relationships; possible answer.

1. function
2. degree
3. synonyms
4. category

5. word structure; champion
6. function; operate
7. category; metal
8. antonyms; friendly or humble
9. synonyms; imitate
10. degree; cool or cold

PAGE 41

Answers will vary. Check to see that the second pair of words has the same relationship as the first pair.

PAGE 42

Different references give different spellings for these word elements. The following spellings are taken from *Webster's New World Power Vocabulary* by Elizabeth Morse-Cluley and Richard Read

1. *cardi-*; heart
2. *cosm-*; world
3. *brev-*; short

4. *cent-*; hundred
5. *lucr-*; money
6. *manu-*; hand
7. *vict-*; to conquer
8. *pend-*; to hang
9. *pac-*; peace
10. *junct-*; to join
11. *laud-*; to praise
12. *cap-*; head
13. *pod-*; foot
14. *crypt-*; hidden
15. *flam-*; fire
16. *frater-*; brother
17. *lum-*; light
18. *mob-*; to move

PAGE 43

Choices of words will vary. Here are root meanings:

1. act (action)
2. meter (metric)
3. mar (mariner)
4. frac (fracture)
5. mov, mob (movement, mobile)

6. graph (autograph)
7. phon (symphony)
8. vac (vacant)
9. pater (paternal)
10. sect (intersection)
11. dorm (dormant)
12. sol (solstice)

PAGE 44

Answers will vary.

PAGE 45

1. con; together
2. ab; from
3. omni; all
4. contra; against
5. tele; far
6. ex; out of
7. mill; thousand
8. tetra; four
9. post; after; behind
10. syn; with, together
11. para; beyond

12. super; above
13. circum; around
14. an; not; without
15. com; with
16. ultim; last
17. intra; within
18. meso; medium; middle
19. poly; many
20. equi; same; equal
21. semi; half: part

PAGE 46

Answers will vary.

PAGE 47

1. terrible; terrorize
2. agreement; agreeable
3. childless; childlike
4. artist or artisan; artistic
5. sensory; sensitize
6. redness; reddish
7. neighborly; neighborhood

8. heroism; heroic
9. musical; musician
10. student; studious

PAGE 48

Answers will vary. See meanings of roots and possible answers below.
1. carry (transferable)
2. fire (inflammatory)
3. fast (accelerate)
4. sea (submarine)
5. describe exactly (indefinite)
6. sound (stereophonic)
7. place (dislocation)
8. move (immobile)
9. throw (rejection)
10. carry (exportation)
11. sound (supersonic)
12. skin (epidermal)
13. act (retroactive)
14. talk, say (prediction)
15. average (abnormal)

16. lean, climb (descendant)
17. join (disjunction)
18. take in (reception)
19. push, drive (expulsion)
20. empty (evacuate)
21. not broken (unwholesome)
22. light (illuminate)
23. God (atheism)
24. to tend toward (divergent)
25. people (unpopular)
26. stretch (intensive)
27. follow (consequential)
28. build (destructive)
29. twist (distortion)
30. twirl, spin (disturbance)

PAGE 49

Wording of answers may vary somewhat.
1. causing horror
2. measure around
3. able to move again

Answers

4. like a sphere
5. to cause pain or struggle
6. act of pushing into something
7. pertaining to writing far away
8. one who studies skin
9. causing a burn

PAGE 50

1. *(ante meridiem)* before noon
2. anonymous
3. apartment
4. association
5. assistant
6. attorney
7. calorie
8. department
9. decibel
10. doing business as
11. *(etcetera)* and so on
12. *(exempli gratia)* for example
13. government

14. *(et alii)* and others
15. milliliter
16. versus
17. also known as
18. boulevard
19. *(id est)* that is to say
20. revolutions per minute
21. kilogram

PAGE 51

1. as soon as possible
2. compact disc
3. collect on delivery
4. cardiopulmonary resuscitation
5. district attorney
6. frequently asked questions
7. dead on arrival
8. extrasensory perception
9. recommended daily allowance
10. Federal Bureau of Investigation
11. absent without leave

12. digital video disc
13. intelligence quotient
14. Internal Revenue Service
15. prisoner of war
16. registered nurse
17. self-addressed, stamped envelope
18. World Wide Web
19. **s**elf-**c**ontained **u**nderwater **b**reathing **a**pparatus
20. intensive care unit
21. **l**ight **a**mplification by **st**imulated **e**mission of **r**adiation
22. **ra**dio **d**etection **an**d **r**anging
23. **so**und **na**vigation **r**anging
24. zone improvement plan (Code)

PAGE 52

1. stand
2. sea

3. down
4. worm
5. up
6. side
7. ship
8. walk
9. fall
10. out

PAGE 53

1. broken chord
2. slow
3. technically difficult
4. musical work for a solo instrument and orchestra
5. soft
6. spirited
7. composition for solo instrument or solo instrument with piano
8. smooth
9. becoming louder
10. high male voice
11. very loud
12. loudest

13. short interlude
14. short, abrupt rhythm
15. lively
16. without accompaniment

PAGE 54

Answers will vary. See glossary for word meanings.

PAGE 55

See glossary for word meanings.

PAGE 56

Demonstrations will vary. See glossary for word meanings.

PAGE 57

Answers will vary. Examine student answers to make sure they find a reasonable contradiction in each example.

PAGE 58

1. top spot
2. lion oil

3. No lemons no melons
4. a SANTA at NASA
5. party trap
6. Was it a bat I saw?
7. Ana, nab a banana.
8. Del saw a sled.
9. Step on no pets.
10. Do geese see God?
11. Wonton? Not now.
12. straw warts

PAGE 59

1. **amphibious** should be **ambidextrous**
2. **neutrons** should be **croutons**
3. **distinguisher** should be **extinguisher**
4. **illegible** should be **eligible**
5. **pheasants** should be **peasants**
6. **irritation** should be **irrigation**

7. **cursing** should be **cruising**
8. **contraptions** should be **contractions**
9. **pineapple** should be **pinnacle**
10. **thesaurus** should be **tyrannosaurus**, and **bronchitis** should be **brontosaurus**

PAGE 60

Answers will vary.

PAGE 61

1. yes
2. Answers will vary.
3. Answers will vary.
4. natatorium
5. Answers will vary.
6. Answers will vary.

PAGE 62

Answers will vary. See glossary for word meanings.

PAGE 63

Answers will vary.

PAGE 64

Statements will vary. See definitions for each word to help determine if student answers are correct.

1. aneurysm — dangerous bulging blood vessel.
2. metastasize — spread from one part of the body to another
3. hemorrhage — excessive bleeding
4. gastroenteritis — inflammation of the stomach or intestines
5. pericardium — lining around the heart
6. arteriosclerosis — hardening of the arteries
7. hematoma — a mass of blood formed as the result of a broken blood vessel

Answers

8. hypoglycemia — low blood sugar
9. hepatitis — liver disease
10. carcinogenic — cancer-causing
11. toxins — poisons
12. benign — not malignant
13. podiatrist — food doctor
14. encephalogram — printed measurement of electrical activity of the brain
15. biopsy — surgical removal of tissue for examination

PAGE 65

Explanations will vary somewhat. Be sure the student has gained the general idea of the meaning of the idiom.

PAGE 66

1. swans
2. bats
3. aircraft
4. leopards
5. caterpillars
6. clams
7. angels
8. dolphins
9. bears
10. crocodiles
11. mosquitoes
12. coyotes
13. kangaroos
14. arrows
15. beavers
16. kittens
17. crows
18. foxes
19. asteroids
20. whales
21. peacocks
22. hens
23. baboons
24. camels

PAGE 67

If a ninety degree angle is right, are all other angles wrong?

PAGE 68

Did Betsy Ross's friends call her Miss Sew-and-Sew?

PAGE 69

1. up
2. fly
3. board
4. bean
5. cheese
6. down
7. ship
8. dust
9. gate
10. drum
11. thumb
12. cat
13. moon
14. water

PAGE 70

Answers will vary.

PAGE 71

Answers will vary.

PAGE 72

1. tears
2. epitaphs
3. leopard
4. Texas
5. smiles
6. sever
7. percussion
8. antlers
9. article
10. vowels
11. the classroom

PAGE 73

1. bee's knees
2. rare chair
3. loud crowd

4. wrong song
5. glib fib
6. middle fiddle
7. quicker vicar
8. lovin' oven
9. wider spider
10. nickel pickle
11. other mother
12. duller color
13. teachers' bleachers
14. mellow fellow
15. wiser miser
16. vanilla gorilla
17. sinister minister
18. president's residence

PAGE 74
Answers will vary.

PAGE 75
1. a square meal
2. cut loose
3. read between the lines

4. split hairs
5. crossfire
6. foreign language
   (four IN language)
7. You're under arrest.
8. long time, no see (no C)

PAGE 76
1. once (ones) upon a time
2. odds are against you
3. settle down
4. ring around the rosie
5. just in case
6. head over heels
7. time after time (or double time)
8. long underwear

PAGE 77
Answers will vary.
Traditional completions are:
1. fish, visitors
2. lie in it

3. the devil you don't
4. death and taxes
5. honor
6. shouldn't throw stones
7. skeleton
8. Rome
9. water
10. spite your face
11. fire
12. fences
13. pay the piper (or fiddler)
14. mustard

PAGE 78
1. lethal; lethargic
2. obstruct; obtrude
3. spy; squab
4. clarinet, clarion
5. bonkers, bonito
6. banshee, bantam

PAGE 79
1. your slip is showing

2. to the mall and do
   some shopping
3. trail snacks
4. a crushing blow
5. do your chores
6. pack of lies
7. tumbling rocks
8. people think I am
   not too smart

PAGE 80
Answers will vary.

PAGE 81
1. for peeping
   during a test
2. because he was
   a little hoarse
3. because their bills
   are over dew
4. anything but crew cuts
5. because there are just
   too many cheetahs
6. It got toad (towed)